7 secrets to a happy and healthy marriage...

The 5th one will blow you away

Introductio n

Assuming you are hitched, you might have found the reason why marriage is so important and encountered a portion of the decency that comes from it. Or then again, perhaps marriage was hard for some of you and you're not generally hitched. In any case, there is trust. In any case, that trust begins with understanding that marriage can be surprisingly astounding.

I've been hitched numerous years and have encountered both the astounding as well as the exceptionally hard. Marriage disposed of depression for myself as well as my better half. We are more powerful in functioning as a group as opposed to filling in as people. Through challenges, we have both developed. Furthermore, a side extra, we have magnificent children that came from our association. Those are completely fine and superb, however I've additionally found something significantly more prominent. I accept God has made union with uncover more about Him and how marvelous He is. Also, this is uncovered through a considerable lot of His motivations for marriage

CHAPTER 1

Reality with regards to marriage

Marriage is the start — the start of the family — and is a long lasting responsibility. It additionally gives a chance to fill in benevolence as you serve your better half and kids. Marriage is in excess of an actual association; it is likewise a profound and close to home association. This association reflects the one among God and His Church.Everyone needs a cheerful marriage, and blissful relationships are generally excellent! In any case, bliss isn't what makes marriage generally lovely. This might come as a shock, or you might know precisely where I'm going with this. One way or the other, I want to believe that you learn something as you read on.

I have had to deal with bounty... bounty great and bounty terrible.

We've encountered both in view of things we did (we've used sound judgment and unfortunate ones), and furthermore as a result of reasons beyond our reach. You can presumably say something similar, truth be told!.

Each marriage has highs and lows. In any case, for what reason do we remain together through everything? Is it to overcome the difficult situations to partake in the great times? Or then again is it something different?

Chapter 2

What makes marriage work

What is the one irreplaceable element for making relationships work? Day to day life instructors normally reply: correspondence. This is uplifting news, in light of the fact that powerful correspondence can be learned. Abilities like undivided attention, utilizing "I" proclamations, focusing on my sentiments and those of my life partner, and learning tips for "battling fair" make marriage more straightforward. A few couples utilize these abilities naturally in light of the fact that they saw them demonstrated in their own childhood. Others can learn them through classes, studios and perusing.

Obviously, the hardest piece of imparting generally comes when there is conflict among you.

Responsibility and Common Values

A few fixings, if missing, can destine a relationship all along. Two essential ones are responsibility and normal qualities.

Responsibility bonds a couple together when you are drained, irritated, or irate with one another. In some cases, recalling your commitments can provoke you to push past these issues and attempt to pardon and begin once more.

Normal qualities are significant. In the event that you're not together on fundamental qualities like kids, genuineness, constancy, and investing family before energy, no measure of learning or exertion of the will can determine the contention. For instance, consistent strain will result assuming that one companion needs to live essentially while different needs life's extravagances.

Otherworldliness/Faith

You probably won't see yourself as an otherworldly individual; in any case, anybody who looks for the more profound significance of life, and not a daily existence zeroed in on private joy, works out of a profound sense. For some this want is communicated in obligation to a particular confidence custom. Here one gets together with others to love God and work for a long term benefit.

In spite of the fact that being an individual of confidence isn't vital for making your marriage work, it's a reward. Surely great individuals all through the ages have had blissful relationships and not every one of them have been strict. Be that as it may, it assists with having confidence standards to direct you and a confidence local area to energize your responsibility.

Now and again people and couples can feel disappointed, miserable and unfulfilled in their relationships/connections and be uncertain with regards to what precisely is off-base

There are many variables that add to a delightful marriage/relationship, for example, Love, Commitment, Trust, Time, Attention, Good Communication including Listening , Partnership, Tolerance, Patience, Openness, Honesty, Respect, Sharing, Consideration, Generosity, Willingness/Ability to Compromise, Constructive administration of Disagreements/Arguments, Willingness to see another's perspective, Ability and Willingness to Forgive/Apologize,

Fun. The rundown is straightforward and self-evident yet it tends to be truly challenging for people/couples to reestablish their marriage/relationship to a fantastic one when hardships emerge or when they float separated.

There are numerous areas of closeness that can upgrade a marriage/relationship, assist it with staying solid and assist it with refocusing when it has become far off/troublesome. Some of the time couples feel that things are not right between them, they can't help thinking about what's up and what they can do?

The accompanying four areas of closeness can assist with directing a couple in surveying how their relationship is and can likewise direct a couple in how to turn out to be nearer and further develop their relationship when hardships emerge, or when they have become far off from each other.

Areas of Closeness

Doing things Together.   Physical Closeness

Profound Closeness.   Sexual Closeness

None of the four regions above are a higher priority than one another yet each can assist one more region with flourishing and all together they can assist a relationship with turning out to be really fulfilling, closer, more private

Doing Things Together

Couples really must get to know one another. With occupied lives, numerous responsibilities and kids to really focus on couples can wind up with next to no time for one another. Hanging out routinely, shopping, feasting out, going to the film, strolling, swimming,involvement in sports, working out, sharing leisure activities and occasions can help couples become nearer and have additional opportunity to talk and hence get to know each other better.

Actual Closeness

A couple must be close genuinely. This can incorporate eye to eye connection, clasping hands, embracing, sitting near one another, rubbing each other. More open doors for actual closeness will improve a couple's feeling of closeness and closeness.

Couples genuinely should be cognizant that a few people are more happy with being truly expressive than others and it means quite a bit to attempt to grasp how agreeable or generally your mate/accomplice is and take it from that point.

Profound Closeness

Profound closeness will assist couples with getting to be aware and see each other all the more profoundly and furthermore have compassion for one another. It includes opening up to one another about sentiments, considerations, convictions, values, trusts, stresses, fears, dreams and aspirations. Mindful listening improves profound closeness when the two people tune in to get to be aware and figure out their mate/accomplice all the more completely, as opposed to deviate, judge, fault oror scrutinize their companion/accomplice.

Sexual Closeness

It is vital that the two people are content with their couple sexual relationship and feel ready to raise and examine their sexual relationship with the other depending on the situation. Some of the time couples can be extremely worried about the recurrence of their sexual action. However long the two people are content with the recurrence and the idea of their sexual movement there is no requirement for them to be concerned or to contrast their sexual relationship with those depicted in the media or those announced by others of their associate, the two of which can be at difference with the real world.

To best comprehend how a marriage can break into pieces, it is useful first to a portion of the manners in which that solid relationships are organized, and the way that they capability.

Solid marriage accomplices are viable accomplices

In a marriage that is to go the distance, sentiment is significant, yet similarity is basic. Overall, relationships will generally be populated by accomplices who come to their marriage with previous critical compatibilities (of character, personality, objectives, and so on) that make it more straightforward for them to arrive at arrangement since they every now and again wind up needing exactly the same thing. They might impart shared traits to respect to character, demeanor, or inclinations for unpredictable or struggle staying away from communications, as well as objectives, strict and moral goals, and so on.

While these areas of arrangement really do will generally be available in sound relationships, we ought to take note of that no marriage is great, and that numerous entirely great relationships harbor conflicts as to a portion of the spaces we've examined. As a rule, in any case, the more spaces you and your accomplice are in settlement on, the better are your opportunities for a sound marriage.

Foundation factors assume a minor part in deciding marriage achievement.

Character, disposition and objective similarity is vital in deciding if a marriage will areas of strength for be. Other foundation factors are additionally significant, notwithstanding. Better relationships are accounted for by individuals who decided to wed further down the road rather than more youthful, by individuals who was seriously enamored with their accomplices before getting hitched, and by individuals who keep up with close family connections and whose guardians' supported their marriage. Likewise, individuals related to more conventional sex-job and strict qualities will quite often report having greater relationships by and large (in spite of the fact that obviously such individuals aren't simply detailing positive results in view of their craving to introduce themselves in a positive light). At the point when all variables connecting with conjugal change are viewed as together, character and labor of love similarity is by all accounts of foremost significance, and foundation factors, for example, whether accomplices come from comparative family, strict or financial foundations or whether they have comparable dating chronicles give off an impression of being of lessor significance.

Chapter3

Importance of marriage

1. Starting

"Marriage is in excess of an actual association; it is likewise a profound and close to home association."

Marriage is the start — the start of the family — and is a deep rooted responsibility. It additionally gives a chance to fill in magnanimity as you serve your better half)and kids. Marriage is in excess of an actual association; it is likewise an otherworldly and profound association. This association reflects the one among God and His Church.

2. Unity

At the point when a man and lady get hitched, the "two become one." Marriage is a bond like no other. It gives us a soul mate, a colleague, as we travel through the difficulties of coexistence.

3. Virtue

Marriage is intended for virtue. We face enticement essentially consistently and from all headings. The obligation of marriage gives us the help to overcome enticement by taking part in profound, fulfilling love — an affection that provides for, and gets from, our mate genuinely, inwardly, and profoundly.

4. Nurturing

At the point when a marriage creates a kid or gets a kid through reception, it is quite possibly of life's most prominent gift. Generally 40% of youngsters being brought today are up in a home without a dad. The impacts of that reality are faltering. Father nonappearance causes expansions in mental and social problems as well as crime and substance misuse. Yet, when youngsters are brought up in a solid marriage, they get an unparalleled view to see and experience the enduring advantages of serious areas of strength for a.

5. Love

Marriage is intended to reflect our Creator's unrestricted love for us. An adoration won't necessarily be there and will ever leave us or spurn us. At the point when a man and lady love each other genuinely, satisfaction and bliss follow.

6. It benefits everybody: Marriage gives a few benefits to both you and others around you. It advances social union and even contributes monetarily to the general public. Marriage likewise helps the two accomplices' families and lays out another connection between two individuals.

7.It shows you empathy: Why is marriage so significant? Since marriage shows the two accomplices sympathy and permits them to try it. It develops your bond by expecting you to stay with another through various challenges. It likewise empowers you to help each other in all that happens, and it is a heap of shared feeling filled the development of a family in light of sympathy and love.

8. Shared association: What is the significance of marriage? It interfaces you to another spirit and permits you to impart everything to them. You might

discuss anything you desire without stressing over being reprimanded or excused to them. This connection gives you a dearest companion who will stay close by in all sorts of challenges.

9.   Organization: Marriage likewise permits you to see one more soul as your own. That explains why marriage is so significant and why it is the most sacred   relationship.   You're dearest companions, darlings, and even sidekicks with this

person. You'll have an individual to hold while you're feeling down, somebody to eat dinner with, and even somebody to watch films with. It is difficult to be forlorn when you have your sidekick. Both of you might go on trips, eat in the mornings, and, surprisingly, read books together.

You won't ever be separated from everyone else after you wed. Marriage is the association of two people that permits you to do a wide range of wonderful things to even the most interesting of individuals. You might live it up with your soul mate the entire constantly and never feel forlorn.

10. Closeness: Marriage additionally enjoys the benefit of permitting you and your companion to be cozy at whatever point you want. It permits you to have a faultless evening of deviousness without stressing over whether you made the best choice. With marriage, you will actually want to communicate your closeness

without feeling regretful or harming God.

11. Profound security: Marriage is the association of two individuals' feelings. All kinds of people are continuously searching for profound association and strength, and this is precisely exact thing you get when you get hitched. You will constantly have somebody to impart your feelings to. The superb thing about marriage is that everything is spotless; regardless of what you

do, there is no debasement or disgrace in this association.

12.They Feel Defensive Around One Another

Do you observe that you're continually strolling around your home with your dukes up? It could be a sign separation is close. As indicated by Bilek, a characteristic condition of preventiveness around your life partner is a terrible sign.

"Companions who are continually wary for an assault from one another are in a terrible spot," he says. "Normally, the assaults are difficult for the marriage, yet the guarded reactions can be similarly unsafe. Answering with preventiveness to your life partner causes them to feel unheard and detached and sets up a pattern of heightening that can eventually obliterate the relationship."

13.One Partner Refuses to Talk

Inside and out quietness is generally a terrible sign. It could prompt separation soon, particularly in the event that one accomplice is truly attempting to suss out a relationship's issues. "Assuming that you attempt to draw in your life partner on the issues that are irritating you, and all you get is quietness, closing down, or looking at, your relationship isn't in a decent spot," adds Bilek. "Stalling is [a] terrible sign. It implies that somebody has stopped investing energy into fixing things. Also, in the event that that work isn't there, things will just deteriorate."

14.They Always Criticize Each Other

Without a doubt, a little useful analysis can be useful in practically any part of your life. In any case, it just works with balance. "On the off chance that you are scrutinizing each other more than you're commending one another, you're set out toward inconvenience," Bilek says. "As a matter of fact, research shows that you want five positive proclamations to balance each regrettable one to keep a relationship enjoying a positive outlook. Steady analysis is one of the significant indications of separation."

15.One Partner Prefers Online Porn to Their Spouse

Generally 50% of relationships end in separate when one accomplice has an "over the top interest in pornography." Bilek makes sense of: "Many individuals watch porn nonchalantly or occasionally. At the point when it turns into a need over a mate, notwithstanding, then it implies that the sexual relationship, and in this manner the marriage, is seriously compromised. The vast majority are troubled taking on a supporting role to the PC, and when it's in this delicate domain, it can detonate a relationship before long."

16.They Are Choosing Online Relationships Over Their Spouse

At the point when people focus on internet based connections over the one with their mate, they will generally legitimize it by saying it's not in fact cheating. As per Bilek, "Regardless of whether your web use isn't turning sexual, taking part in heartfelt or coquettish connections online can be tragic for a relationship." He adds, "Profound issues can be basically as disastrous as sexual ones. Assuming you are going to the web to meet a psychological condition you're not getting in your marriage, you might be set out toward separate quicker than you naturally suspect."

17,They Find Themselves Thinking of Other Potential Relationships

This is where things get cloudy. When it's simply you and your considerations, do you fantasize about different connections, and assuming this is the case, is this entrance to unfaithfulness? "It is typical to find others appealing and to feel longing for individuals separated from your life partner," Bilek says. "In any case, when you begin envisioning yourself in a relationship with others and taking into account close subtleties of what that would be like, it's a sign you are shaking off a portion of the obligations of your marriage and puts you on an extremely tricky slant."

18.One — or Both — Is Not Interested in Sex Anymore

See, stuff occurs. Our bodies progress in years, we begin to lose energy, and the fervor of another relationship begins to wear off. Indeed, even your sex drive gets skewed. No real surprise there. "There is no question that over the long haul couples will generally have intercourse less much of the time," says Bilek. "However, in a solid relationship, theaccomplices in sound relationships come to concur upon normal plans with respect to the headings their marriage will take, and the manner in which each accomplice will act. These normal arrangements might very well never have been examined, yet they will be available certainly in how each accomplice decides to act.

Areas of agreement that partners will have dealt with will generally include:

Companionship. Effective accomplices foster a critical companionship at the center of their relationship. They truly like each other, entertain and comfort each other, and really like to invest energy with one another. This kinship and common enjoying is to some degree separate from different parts of the relationship (sexuality, for example), and can endure the deficiency of these different parts of the relationship. A solid fellowship and shared loving is much of the time the reason for fix of disturbed connections.

Job assumptions. The accomplices agree with respect to how family obligations are isolated and the way in which they will act towards one another. Customarily, despite everything overwhelmingly, the male or manly distinguished accomplice will assume most of monetary commitments, while the female or ladylike recognized accomplice will take on sustaining jobs. Custom has separated essentially in the industrialized west over the course of the past 100 years, nonetheless, and it isn't the slightest bit exceptional to find 'ladies' who assume monetary commitments, 'men' who take on supporting jobs, or to find the two accomplices sharing these jobs to some degree. Inability to agree concerning jobs can be a significant wellspring of contention.

Profound closeness. Fruitful accomplices figure out how to trust one another, to be open to one another, to giggle together, and to help each other in the midst of hardship.

Sexual assumptions. Accomplices come to essential arrangements concerning how they will be sexual with one another.

Habitually (generally) this implies that they will be sexual with each other, and not with others, but rather this isn't really the situation. Sexual assumptions might additionally direct the sorts and examples of sexual exercises that each accomplice endlessly won't participate in. Coming to concurrence concerning sexuality can increment believe that couples feel for one another, and inability to arrive at understanding can be cause for struggle. As sexual movement is emphatically fulfilling and holding for couples, it is best for relationships when accomplices concur upon sexual assumptions and are both happy with their lovemaking.

Vision/Goals. Fruitful accomplices concur that they need to seek after similar life ways, values and objectives and commonly focus on those ways, values and objectives. Models could incorporate choices to have kids or not, to join in or not go to strict administrations, to raise a child or notCloseness in your relationship is low to such an extent that the actual closeness isn't even of interest any longer, that is a terrible sign."

19.One Person Has an Addiction and Isn't Seeking Treatment

Addictions are relationship executioners. Truth be told, almost 50% of connections end in separate when somewhere around one accomplice has a compulsion. "While getting your substance of decision is more critical to you than your life partner, it is inevitable before your decisions push you endlessly further away from them," Bilek says. "An individual drank by getting their next drink or their next high won't ever have the important energy to give to the relationship."

20.One Partner Refuses to Attend Counseling

As indicated by research by the American Association of Marriage and Family Therapists, an incredible 97% of couples overviewed expressed that external assistance got their relationships in the groove again. Along these lines, marriage mentoring and couples treatment work. Be that as it may, provided that a couple really goes. "Anything that the issue is, assuming that you have been not able to settle it all alone, an expert couples instructor can help tremendously," Bilek says. "The demonstration of essentially going to directing is a declaration of your obligation to one another. Thus, when one accomplice will not go to meetings, it's an indication that they are reluctant to invest the essential energy into the marriage. What's more, regardless of whether the issue is little, you could be confronting a serious disintegration of the relationship."

Chapter 4

7 secret strategies to a happy and healthy marriage

Don't you want to know the mystery ingredient to a blissful and durable marriage, particularly from those joyfully hitched couples who have aced the specialty of driving a cheerful relationship?

I will disclose keys to a fruitful marriage that will help you issue settle the conjugal issues, incapacitate the clashing accomplice and help you make and keep an effective marriage.

Whether you are a love bird or allude to yourselves as 'old Ball 'n' Chain,' each marriage has its portion of high points and low points. While it might sound banality, respites and examples of ordinariness are normal to the back and forth movement of hitched life.

Times of pressure, fatigue, and unfortunate correspondence are essential for the course.

"Marriage takes work."

Marriage accomplishes take work, and like anything more throughout everyday life, you need to accomplish the work to receive the benefit. Yet, crafted by marriage isn't similar to cleaning the latrine and making a garbage run.

Marriage is an association of two spirits, yet the importance of fruitful marriage varies from one couple to another. There is no reasonable meaning of a fruitful marriage. Be that as it may, here are a few standard meanings of a fruitful

1.Unconditional love and understanding

One more typical meaning of a fruitful marriage is responsibility, obligation, and penance. Certain individuals accept that great comprehension and unrestricted love are the keys to a fruitful marriage. Acknowledge each other imperfections

2. Defining Limits

One more significant key to an effective marriage is defining individual limits decisively. You ought to keep a singular life and carve out some margin for yourself. You might be going on dates for five days every week, except you ought to likewise have the option to meet with your loved ones.

The most effective method to define limits

1. Utilize Clear Communication. Invest energy recognizing what means a lot to you in your

relationship and your life. What "slope would you say you will pass on" and what are you ready to be more adaptable about? Whenever you've distinguished your particular limits, utilize clear language while examining them with your partner:"Please don't speed when I'm a traveler in our vehicle."

"If it's not too much trouble, regard my protection."

"I'm not OK with raised voices during struggle."

"Strain to have intercourse makes me anxious."

"I really want a half-hour to myself when I return home from work to de-pressurize and better assistance with the children."

Plunk down with your accomplice to examine your qualities, express your requirements, and concur upon limits that will maintain these necessities. Ensure these are limits you are both arranged to regard and respect.

2. Set Clear Consequences. When you and your accomplice have examined your limits — the "musts" and "must nots" your relationship should find success — the following stage is to be clear about what the results are if and when limits aren't regarded.

For instance, assuming you and your life partner concur that you won't speak loudly during struggle, a result of shouting during a battle could be stopping the contention and going for a 30-minute stroll alone.

You genuinely must completion on the outcomes of any limit infringement. Not totally finishing shows your accomplice that you don't regard your own limits — and in the event that you don't regard your limits, for what reason would it be advisable for them?

3. Assume Liability. Keep in mind: Everything you do and say has a characteristic outcome, whether positive or negative. For instance, assuming you're habitually disparaging of your life partner, they presumably won't have any desire to get physically involved with you. However, on the off chance that you talk generous and cease from shouting during a contention, they're bound to have a real sense of safety and want actual closeness and association.

3. Acknowledgment

A significant relationship executioner, absence of acknowledgment, is a characteristic all the more normally credited to ladies known for their irritating. Keep in mind, you wedded your accomplice for who he was then and presently. Regardless of whether we needed to transform him now, we can't.

The way in to an effective marriage lies in understanding this at the earliest opportunity.

While encouraging or convincing him, you just spotlight on his shortcomings or issues. Alter your point of view right away and begin zeroing in on certain qualities all things considered.

.

4.. Keep closeness alive

Sex is vital to a sound marriage. Sex ought to be customary, and advisors recommend doing it in any event, when you're not in that frame of mind!

We propose keeping it intriguing by discussing what satisfies you and adding any dream pretending, positions, or room props you might need to acquaint with keep it energizing.

All things considered, what is a fruitful marriage on the off chance that it doesn't allow you to get what you want?

Life mentor Giovanni Maccarrone discusses how pursuing this one cognizant choice prior to getting hitched can assist with making a marriage fruitful.

12 Ways to keep closeness alive

1 Be liberal. This doesn't mean purchasing your accomplice wonderful things and going a

little overboard on costly dinners. It alludes to being liberal when you part with yourself. Be liberal when you share your time and sentiments with your accomplice. Try not to waste time with mind games that include who will say sorry first, who ought to get the telephone to ask the other out on the town first, etc.

Recollect that being involved with somebody is about compromise, so try not to keep track of who's winning with regards to the awful things. Despite the fact that being liberal is vital, consistently make sure to keep a feeling of uniqueness when you are seeing someone. The greatest no is offering yourself totally and getting up one daytime understanding that you don't have the foggiest idea who you are any longer.

2 Have fun together. Couples that share recreation exercises appreciate more love and less struggle than the people who don't. By participating in

commonly charming exercises, you will feel more associated with your accomplice, in this way producing a more personal connection.

The most effective way to construct closeness is to have some good times together. Whether it is setting out toward laser tag with a gathering of companions, or arranging a heartfelt roof cookout for two, hanging out will without a doubt keep the flash of closeness alive, be it in a new or long haul relationship. [Read: 10 simple tasks to reignite the flash in adoration instantly!]

3 Experience new things together. One more method for building areas of strength for an of closeness with your darling is to enjoy intriguing things together. It very well may be getting away some place neither of you has at any point been to, pursuing a cooking class, or going through the early evening time

rollerblading together interestingly.

By encountering new things together, both of you are establishing the groundwork in your bid to construct a more prominent feeling of network and closeness with one another. In addition to that, your victories and disappointments while endeavoring these new exercises will add to the abundance of recollections that you two are accumulating together.

4 Prove your affection. Nothing is more close than demonstrating to your accomplice that you love them. You can pen an adoration letter and leave it in you man's shirt pocket for him to see as later, plan a heartfelt night out for your woman love at her number one clam and champagne bar, or simply tell your accomplice "I Love You" and talk from the heart. Regardless of what you do, your accomplice will see the value in the time and exertion that you put into

demonstrating your friendship and love.

#5 Communicate unreservedly. Do whatever it takes not to maintain any mysteries from one another if possible. Indeed, a harmless exaggeration to a great extent never hurt anybody, yet it is in every case best to be straightforward with the individual you care about. On the off chance that you think he went with a terrible choice putting resources into that specific block of offers, then let him know your thought process. In the event that you think it isn't up to her to castigate her associate, then tell her so.

Indeed, reality might damage and start a minor conflict, yet by the day's end, your accomplice will thank you for tell the truth. Having the option to discuss uninhibitedly with each other is one of the essentials with regards to keeping closeness alive in a relationship.

6.Allocate date evenings. Keep the flash alive by keeping the energy alive. This is particularly obvious on the off chance that you are burdened with kids, or then again if both of you have occupied professions and not much time for one another. Distribute night out something like one time per week and really try to concentrate the entirety of your consideration and strength on your accomplice.

Play around with one another and relish each other's organization however much you can. Whether it is attempting the new sushi joint down the road, or heading for mixed drinks in the city, guarantee that you put away opportunity to accomplish something significant and fun together

5.. Never utilize the D-word

Assuming you would rather not get a seperation during battle utilize this as a control component. Couples utilizing it threateningly are bound to see Divorce work out as expected Making dangers is definitely not a full grown procedure for tackling any issue, so don't do it.

6.Celebrate little, great, minutes.

"The vast majority of us know that it's vital to show up for our accomplice during the difficult stretches," says Pawelski. Be that as it may, she says, it's similarly as essential to recognize the great times, as well. She expresses that beneficial things really happen more frequently than terrible, however couples frequently botch those chances to interface. So the following time your life partner shares something positive — like a commendation from their chief, "Quickly stop what you are doing and concentrate," she says. "Assist them with appreciating the experience by clarifying pressing issues and effectively commending the uplifting news." In doing as such, you'll show appreciation for the blissful minutes in your marriage.

Chapter 5

Figuring out how to cope with common marriage problems

While you're managing issues in your marriage, it can some of the time feel like you're in isolation. Luckily, there are numerous ways you can speak with your companion and think of answers for tackle your concerns together. We've incorporated a rundown of ways you can adapt to your marriage issues to chat with your accomplice and work toward fixing your relationship, mindfully.

1 Communicate about issues in your relationship.

Open correspondence is the way in to any solid relationship. You and your accomplice need to discuss any battles you're going through.When you let things go or expect they'll get better all alone, they will generally putrefy, which can prompt hatred over the long run. At the point when you notice issues springing up, put your life partner down and talk with them about it. You can raise issues in the relationship by expressing something like, "Hello honey, might we at any point plunk down and talk sometime tonight? I have a couple of things I might want to visit with you about, just to ensure we're in total agreement."

To try not to put your life partner on edge, use "I" explanations. [3] For example, rather than saying, "You generally get back home late," you could say, "When you stay out late without letting me know where you're going, I feel stressed."

2lFocus on each issue in turn.

Raising every one of your concerns immediately can feel overpowering. At the point when you plunk down with your accomplice to visit about the thing you're battling with, attempt to pick each thing to discuss in turn. Like that, you can dive profound into a particular issue as opposed to making speculations regarding a lot of things without a moment's delay. For instance, to discuss your closeness (or scarcity in that department) yet in addition about your feelings of anxiety, pick one and save the other for an alternate time frame.

3.Try to figure out your accomplice's viewpoint.

Listen intently, and make an effort not to intrude. Your accomplice likely has their own perspective on what's happening in your marriage. Give your all to see things according to their point of view, and don't excuse how they're feeling immediately. In the event that you make an honest effort to be understanding, both of you can have better, more useful discussions. Show that you're standing by listening to your accomplice by asking follow-up inquiries like, "Intriguing. Could you at any point let me know more?" or, "I don't know I comprehend. Might you at any point make sense of that once more?"

4.Come up with arrangements together.

The objective is to arrive at a choice that benefits both of you. Regardless of whether it's an issue that only one of you is having, you ought to attempt to arrive at a mutually beneficial arrangement: something that causes you both to feel like you're working on your relationship and developing nearer together. This might take a short time, and you could need to talk on different occasions with your life partner, yet eventually, everything will work out just fine.

For example, assuming the issue is that you believe you do a greater number of errands around the house than your life partner does, you could make a task list that you both work on over time. Like that, you can both perceive the number of errands you two that are doing, and you both feel like you're similarly adding to the family.

5.Accept the things you can't change about your accomplice.

There might be repeating issues that harvest up over the long haul. This can seem like a warning, yet as a general rule, it's typical for most long haul connections. You and your accomplice will most likely differ about comparable things a great deal, and that is completely fine. Significantly, you stay deferential and kind while tending to these conflicts, whether it's the initial time or the 50th time.

For instance, perhaps you like to tidy up the house toward the finish of every day, while your accomplice likes to do a major cleanup toward the week's end. Both of you could examine this much over your relationship, yet it's not really something terrible — it's simply a distinction in inclinations.

6.Forgive your accomplice if possible.

Clinging to outrage and disdain isn't perfect for your marriage. Assuming you feel hurt or distraught at your accomplice actually, work on excusing them for the past. Ensure you've completely talked through the issue, and attempt to get a genuine statement of regret from your accomplice, in the event that they're willing. Then, you can pick whether you can excuse your companion to keep the relationship pushing ahead.

Recall that absolution isn't let your accomplice know that their activities are alright — it's permitting yourself to continue on as opposed to clinging to old sentiments.

7.Divide family undertakings.

Division of work is a tremendous disputed matter in many connections. Frequently, the two accomplices feel as they're accomplishing practically everything, so they begin to get angry. Plunk down with your mate and discuss who does what around the house, and roll out certain improvements assuming that there are any issues.

It could assist with making a rundown of what the both of you do step by step. Like that, you can perceive the number of undertakings every one of you that are doing over time.

8.Talk about your nurturing styles.

How you bring up your kids is vital to discuss early. Plunk down with your mate and talk about the particulars of what you might want to do with your kids, and how you'll make it happen. Regardless of whether you concur 100 percent, being in total agreement, about greater issues is significant.

You could express something like, "I believe we must discuss how we'll bring up our kid. Would you like to talk about certain things with me?"

9.Show love to your accomplice consistently.

Express your appreciation for your accomplice at whatever point you can. Give your accomplice an embrace when you return home, get them a tidbit when you're at the store, or send them a sweet message while you're working. These little demonstrations of adoration probably won't seem like a lot, however they can remind you why you experienced passionate feelings for in any case.

It helps on the off chance that you know your accomplice's main avenue for affection. For example, in the event that their way to express affection is actual touch, they could see the value in a shoulder rub or a back rub. Or on the other hand, in the event that their way to express affection is help out, you could do a few errands around the house.

10 Make sentiment part of your everyday existence.

Carry on like you're dating your life partner again to bring the flash back. At the point when you get overpowered with work, children, and obligations, letting sentiment drop off the radar is simple. Make an honest effort to be heartfelt toward your accomplice so you both recall what it seemed like when you initially began dating.You could:

Eat in bed together

Shock your collaborate with little gifts

Plan an end of the week escape trip

Offer your accomplice praises

Have a candlelit supper at home

11.Remind yourself of your accomplice's positive characteristics.

Zeroing in on the negatives in your relationship can be simple. All things considered, attempt to think of a couple of positive things that your accomplice does:

perhaps they're magnificent at sorting out, or perhaps they are really convenient around the house. Anything it is, regardless of how little, remember those things as you analyze your marriage and your relationship.

On the off chance that it helps, you might make an actual rundown on paper to take a gander at each time you want a shot in the arm. For example, your rundown could say: makes me breakfast on Sundays, is an extraordinary parent, is extremely understanding with the children, is a magnificent cook.

12. Work on yourself.

Look at your own commitments to any issues in the relationship.[It takes two to tango, very much like it takes two to make a marriage work. Regardless of whether you feel like you're totally morally justified, attempt to check out at it according to your accomplice's point of view. Then, you can begin executing little changes in yourself that will prompt greater changes in general.

For example, in the event that you and your mate frequently battle when you need to remain late working, you might be committing a lot of opportunity to your work and insufficient time for your life partner. You could chip away at that by rethinking your timetable and focusing on quality time with your accomplice.

13.Commit 100 percent to your companion.

Ensure you're completely put resources into making your marriage work. In the event that you have all mental energy invested anywhere but here as of now, your marriage issues will most likely just deteriorate. All things considered, advise yourself to take a stab at all that to fix your relationship, regardless of what the result is. In the event that you devote yourself to attempting in your marriage, you're considerably more prone to get to a solid, cheerful spot.

It's normal to begin searching for a "exit plan" of the marriage when circumstances become difficult. Remember, however, that practically all drawn out connections go through difficult times at some point, and the majority of them endure to the opposite side.

14.Focus on different things that satisfy you.

On the off chance that you can't find bliss in your marriage at the present time, track down it in your leisure activities or companions. Relationships once in a while go through difficult situations, and that is fine. Attempt to invest more energy doing things you love, such as spending time with dear companions, plunging into leisure activities, and getting out into nature. Make an effort not to disregard your obligations or your home life (don't pass on your mate to deal with the children consistently), however infuse somewhat fun into your everyday practice to make your life more straightforward.

You can likewise zero in on taking care of oneself and do things that don't require some investment by any means. Endure 10 to 15 minutes absorbing an air pocket shower, perusing a decent book, taking

15. Go to couple's directing assuming you really want to.

Some marriage issues are difficult to fix all alone. A psychological well-being proficient can help you both see each other better and think of arrangements that work for the both of you. On the off chance that you've attempted a couple of things and nothing is working, connect with an expert and make an arrangement.

A couple's instructor can likewise give you genuine, substantial tips to assist you with figuring out through your particular issues as a team.

Conclusion

Carry out what you have been shown in your conjugal life and see uncommon changes.

Made in the USA
Monee, IL
03 October 2022

15104930R00069